Brides in Bloom

Brides in Bloom

Taivo Piller

Photography: Toomas Volkmann

STICHTING KUNSTBOEK

Foreword

I am very proud that you hold this book in your hands!

There are a few things I would like to say, but I promise to make it short
as I would prefer my designs to speak for them.

I have mainly used materials from nature and the fields of Estonia.
These natural materials possess a certain energy and power that I admire:
they are earthy and primal. I have started the project with the very first flowers
that pop out of the snow and I have finished with the last berries of autumn.
The changing seasons play a very important role in my work.

Often people ask me where I get my inspiration from...
That's always a hard question to answer. Of course I am inspired by nature
in the first place, by what I see on my travels, in ancient tribes and in everything
else around me, but I also believe that inspiration can come from imagination
— thinking out new possibilities, techniques, shapes, and considering
previously unused materials.

When you look at the designs it will quickly strike you that in the majority
of the pieces only one kind of botanical material has been used. I had not done
this on purpose and I was quite surprised to discover this, when I was writing
down the list of materials used. It just felt so right for me during the
composition of the work.

I was asking Toomas, the photographer, if there was something that he
would like to focus on and draw the attention to. He said that the most
important thing for him during the process was finding ways to create
the right atmosphere and bringing an impression of air and movement
into the photographs taken in the studio. We worked together to bring
floral photography closer to fashion and design studies in order to create
a frame or background to display the beauty of floral work.

I have always thought that the most important thing about art is
the emotional effect it has on the spectator. Therefore I really hope that
the book will not leave you indifferent!

Taivo Piller

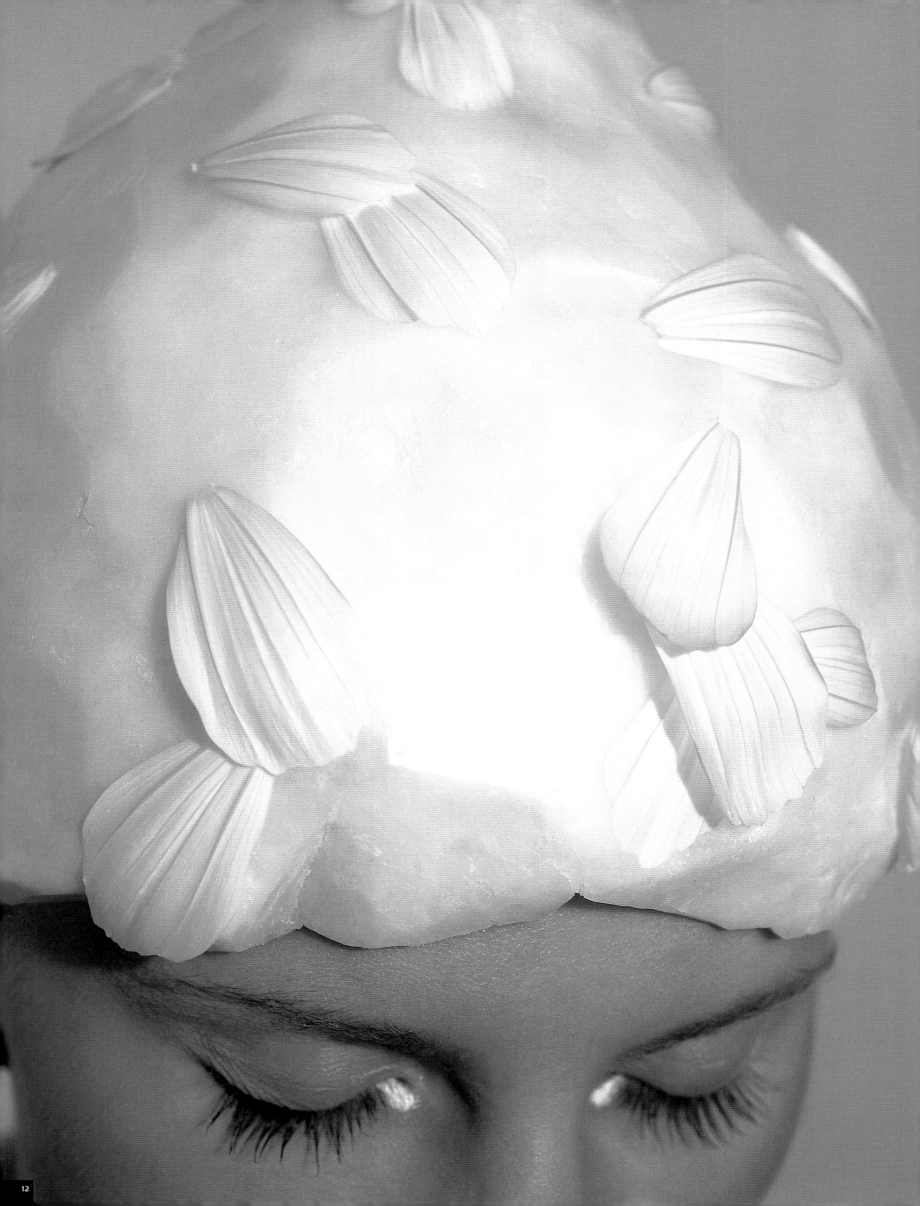

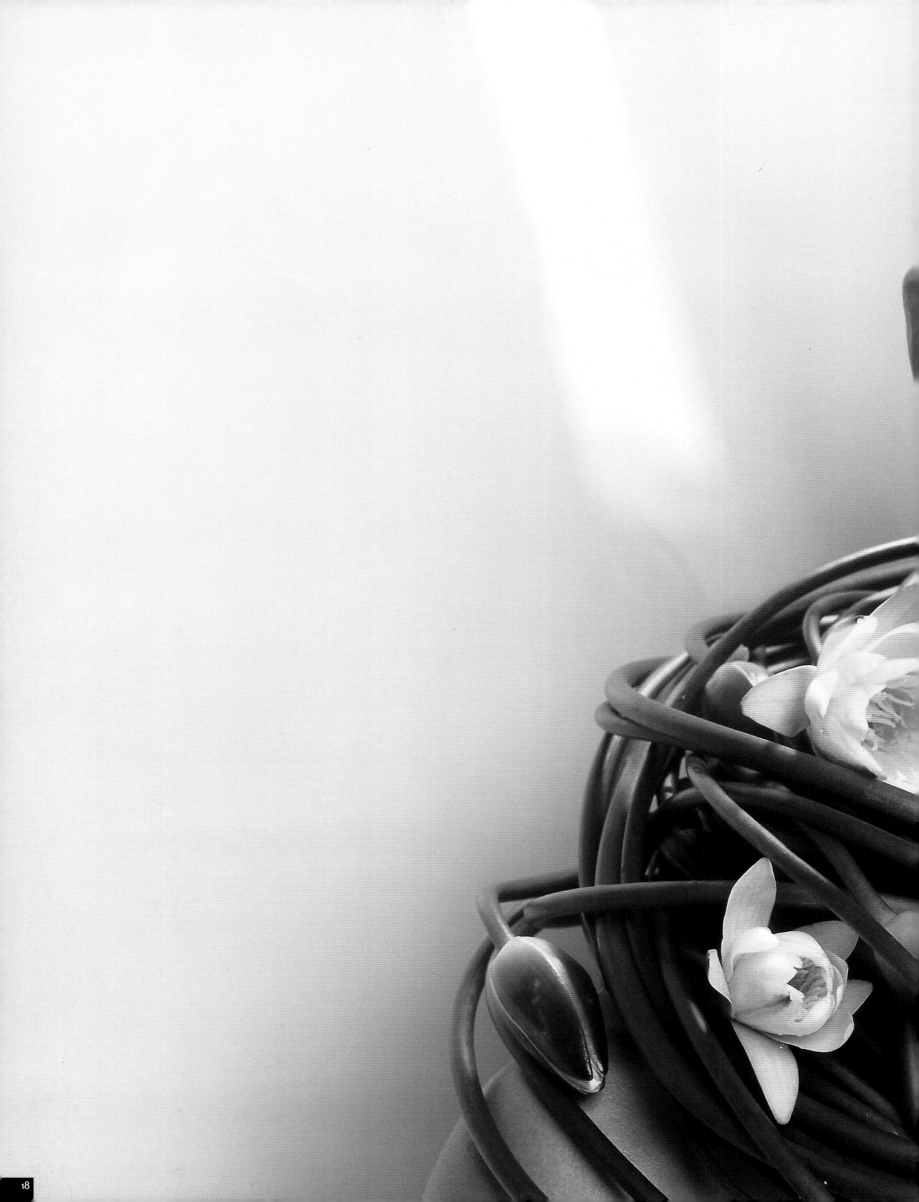

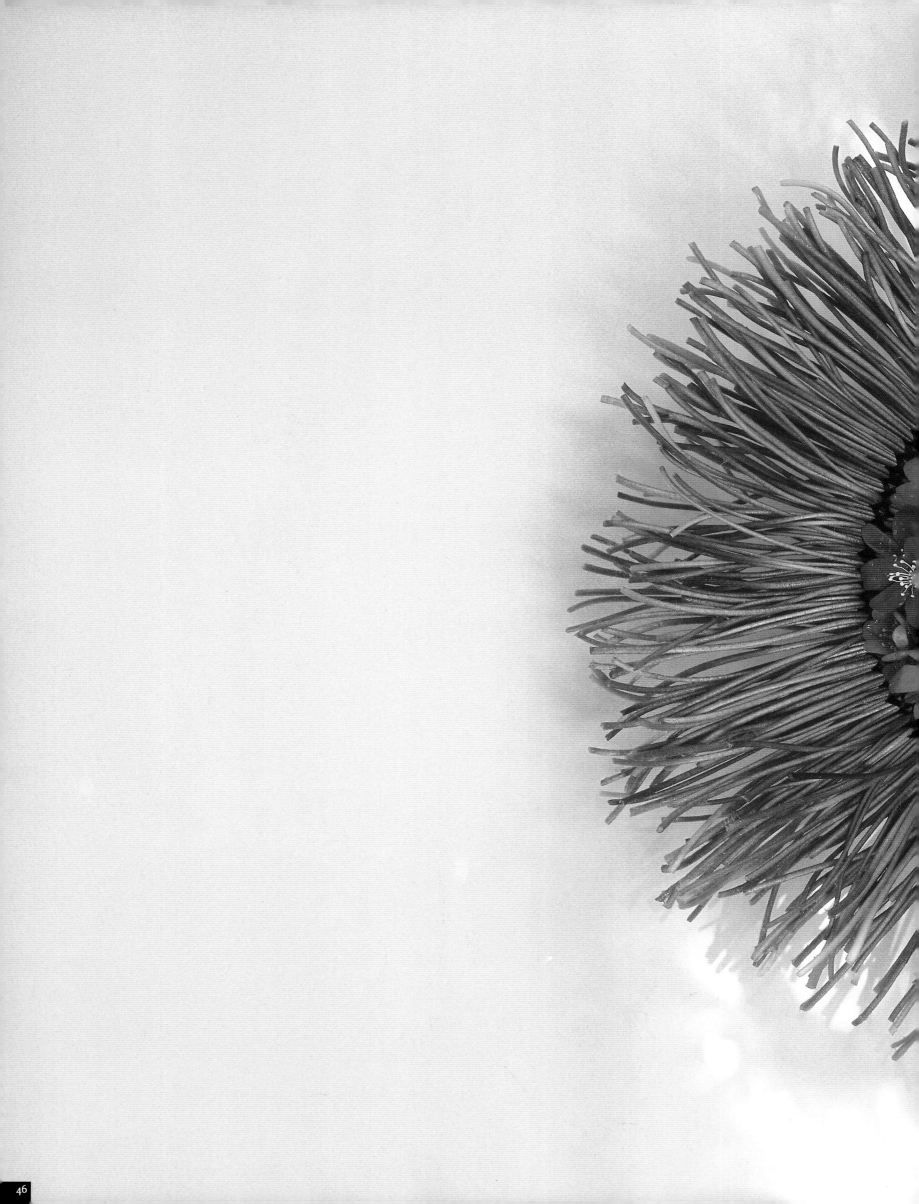

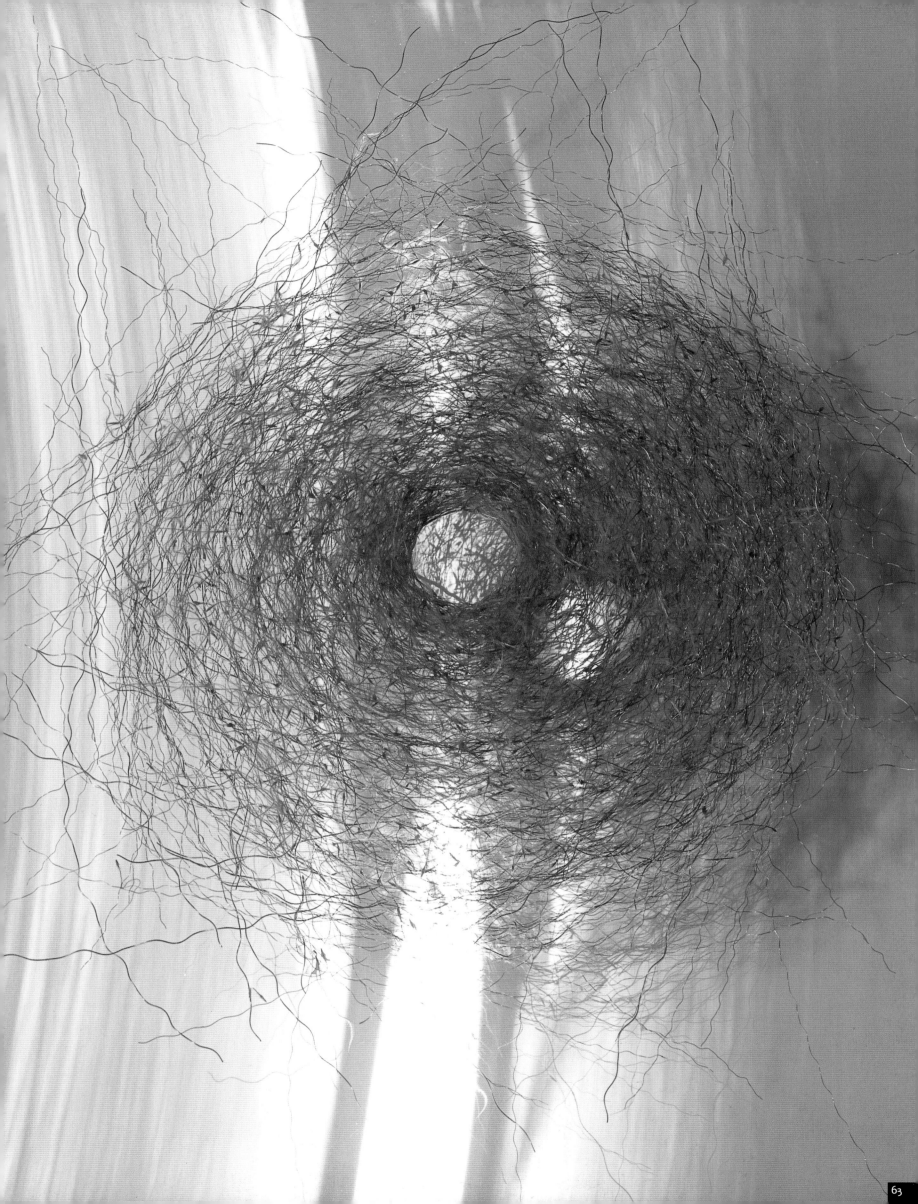

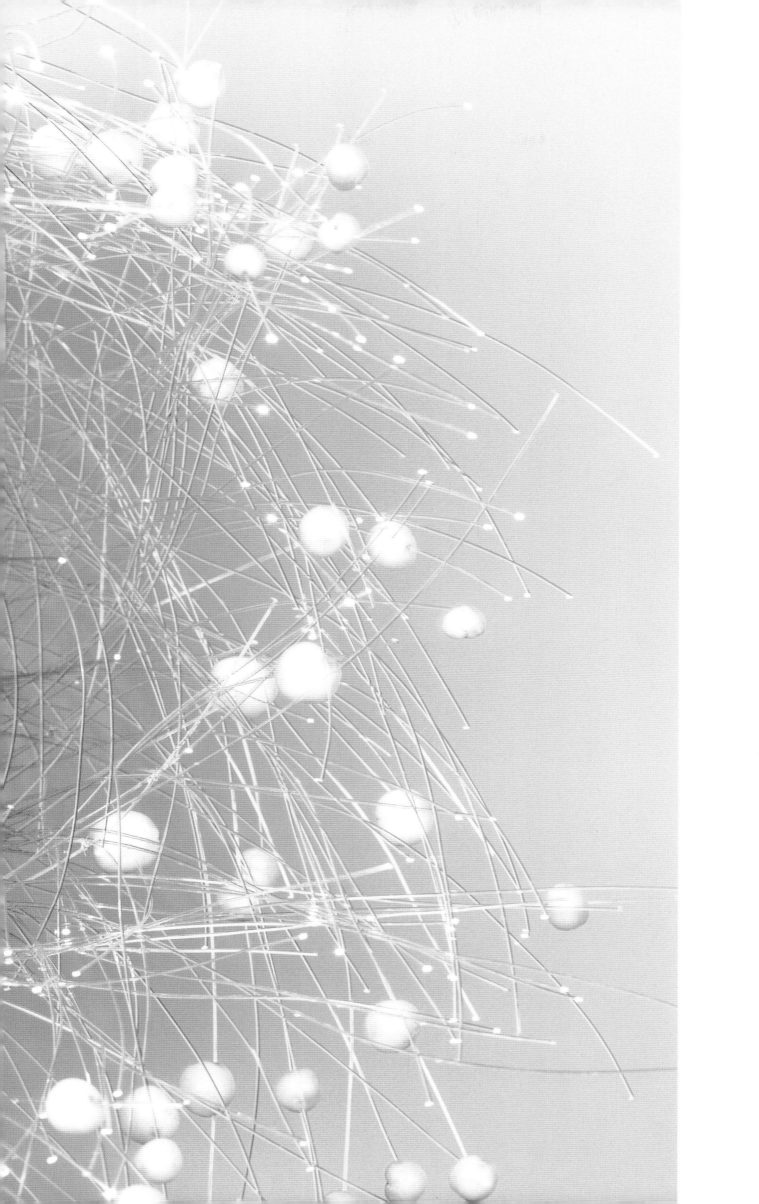

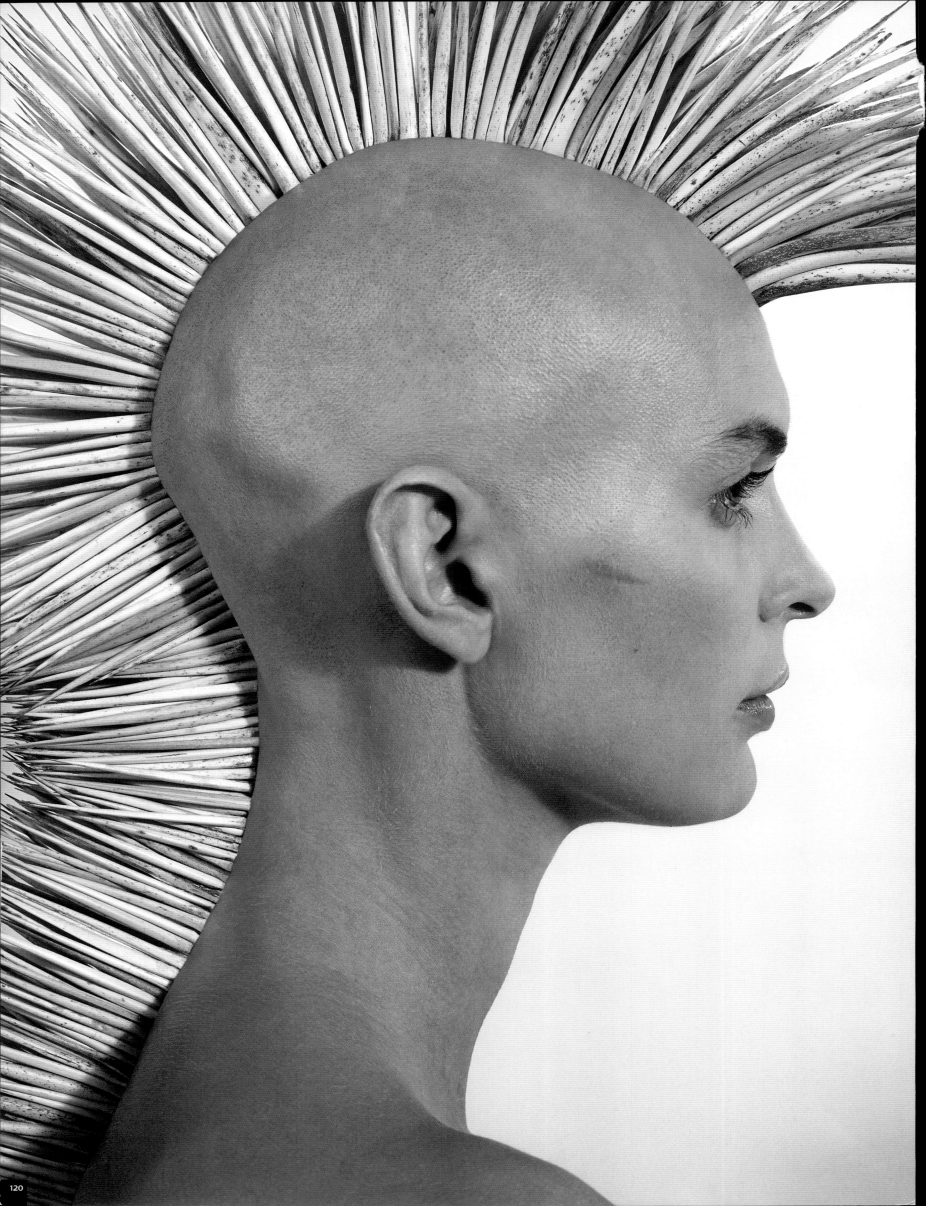